We Can Be Responsible!

WE MAKE LUNCH

By Lynda Arnéz

Gareth Stevens PUBLISHING

Please visit our website, www.garethstevens.com. For a free color catalog of all our high-quality books, call toll free 1-800-542-2595 or fax 1-877-542-2596.

Library of Congress Cataloging-in-Publication Data

Names: Arnéz, Lynda, author.
Title: We make lunch! / Lynda Arnéz.
Description: New York : Gareth Stevens Publishing, [2020] | Series: We can be responsible! | Includes index.
Identifiers: LCCN 2018038788| ISBN 9781538239155 (pbk.) | ISBN 9781538239179 (library bound) | ISBN 9781538239162 (6 pack)
Subjects: LCSH: Luncheons–Juvenile literature. | LCGFT: Cookbooks.
Classification: LCC TX735 .A76 2019 | DDC 642–dc23
LC record available at https://lccn.loc.gov/2018038788

First Edition

Published in 2020 by
Gareth Stevens Publishing
111 East 14th Street, Suite 349
New York, NY 10003

Editor: Kristen Nelson
Designer: Sarah Liddell

Photo credits: Cover, pp. 1, 11 MaKo-studio/Shutterstock.com; p. 5 Sergey Novikov/Shutterstock.com; p. 7 Lopolo/Shutterstock.com; pp. 9, 24 (bread) Gamzova Olga/Shutterstock.com; p. 13 Dmytro Zinkevych/Shutterstock.com; p. 15 Monkey Business Images/Shutterstock.com; pp. 17, 24 (stove) lovemydesigns/Shutterstock.com; pp. 19, 24 (cherries) Robert Kneschke/Shutterstock.com; p. 21 KK Tan/Shutterstock.com; p. 23 Pressmaster/Shutterstock.com.

Printed in the United States of America

CPSIA compliance information: Batch #CS19GS: For further information contact Gareth Stevens, New York, New York at 1-800-542-2595.

Contents

We're hungry!
We can make lunch.

Let's make sandwiches.

I take out bread.

Trin and Nick
cut up lettuce.
They cut tomatoes, too.

Cheyanne makes a
peanut butter sandwich.

Faye makes Mom
a sandwich!

Mia wants soup.
She is careful using
the stove!

We all eat cherries.

Don't forget to clean up!

What can you make for lunch?

Words to Know

bread

cherries

stove

Index